HABITAT SURVIVAL

T0100846

POLAR REGIONS

Melanie Waldron

Raintree

Chicago, Illinois

www.capstonepub.com
Visit our website to find out more information about Heinemann-Raintree books.

To order:

☎ Phone 800-747-4992

▣ Visit www.capstonepub.com
  to browse our catalog and order online.

© 2013 Raintree
an imprint of Capstone Global Library, LLC
Chicago, Illinois

All rights reserved. No part of this publication may be reproduced or transmitted in any form or by any means, electronic or mechanical, including photocopying, recording, taping, or any information storage and retrieval system, without permission in writing from the publisher.

Edited by Nancy Dickmann, Kristen Kowalkowski, and Claire Throp
Designed by Philippa Jenkins
Original illustrations © Capstone Global Library Ltd 2013
Illustrations by Oxford Designers and Illustrators, and Jeff Edwards
Picture research by Tracy Cummins
Originated by Capstone Global Library Ltd

Library of Congress Cataloging-in-Publication Data
Waldron, Melanie.
  Polar regions / Melanie Waldron.
    p. cm.—(Habitat survival)
  Includes bibliographical references and index.
  ISBN 978-1-4109-4599-0 (hb)—ISBN 978-1-4109-4608-9 (pb) 1. Polar regions—Juvenile literature. I. Title.
  G590.W35 2012
  577.0911—dc23   2012000242

Acknowledgments
We would like to thank the following for permission to reproduce photographs: AgeFotostock: Alaska Stock, 14; Alamy: All Canada Photos, 25, Cavan, 20, Steven Kazlowski, Cover, 27, WILDLIFE GmbH, 15; FLPA: Flip Nicklin/Minden Pictures, 18, 22, Samuel Blanc/Biosphoto, 16; Getty Images: Stockbyte, 24; iStockphoto: Keith Szafranski, 23, pilipenkoD, 17; Minden Pictures: Rhinie van Meurs/ NI, 13; Nature Picture Library: Bryan and Cherry Alexander, 21; Shutterstock: Antoine Beyeler, 12, Armin Rose, 26, gary yim, 10, oksana.perkins, 7, Tyler Olson, 5, Vladimir Melnik, 11, Volodymyr Goinyk, 8, Yongyut Kumsri, 29

Every effort has been made to contact copyright holders of any material reproduced in this book. Any omissions will be rectified in subsequent printings if notice is given to the publisher.

Disclaimer
All the Internet addresses (URLs) given in this book were valid at the time of going to press. However, due to the dynamic nature of the Internet, some addresses may have changed, or sites may have changed or ceased to exist since publication. While the author and publisher regret any inconvenience this may cause readers, no responsibility for any such changes can be accepted by either the author or the publisher.

Contents

Some words are shown in bold, **like this**. You can find out what they mean by looking in the glossary.

Frozen Worlds

The polar regions are at the extreme north and south of Earth. The Arctic surrounds the North **Pole** at the very top of the world. The Antarctic, or Antarctica, surrounds the South Pole at the very bottom. Two imaginary lines around Earth—the Arctic Circle and the Antarctic Circle—surround the polar regions.

Day and night

In the polar regions, the Sun never sets in summer. It is sunny all day and all night. In winter, the Sun never rises. There is darkness all day.

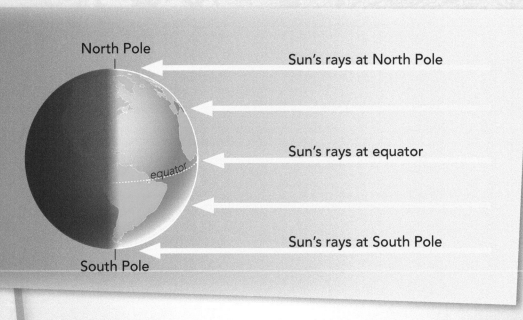

North Pole

Sun's rays at North Pole

Sun's rays at equator

equator

Sun's rays at South Pole

South Pole

Cold poles

The polar regions are cold—very cold. This is because the Sun's rays hit Earth at an angle here, so the heat has to spread out over a large area. Also, the Sun's rays have to travel through more of Earth's **atmosphere** to reach the polar regions. They lose heat doing this.

Polar regions are very cold, windy, and dry. They are known as cold **deserts**.

Polar facts

- Coldest recorded temperature: –129 degrees Fahrenheit (–89.4 degrees Celsius), at the Antarctic
- Average Arctic winter temperature: –29 degrees Fahrenheit (–34 degrees Celsius)

The Arctic

At the North **Pole**, there is no land, only the Arctic Ocean. This ocean is covered by a 10-foot- (3-meter-) thick layer of ice for much of the year. Land from northern countries circles around the edge of the Arctic Ocean. Some of this land forms part of the Arctic polar region. This means that plants and animals from these countries can be found in the Arctic.

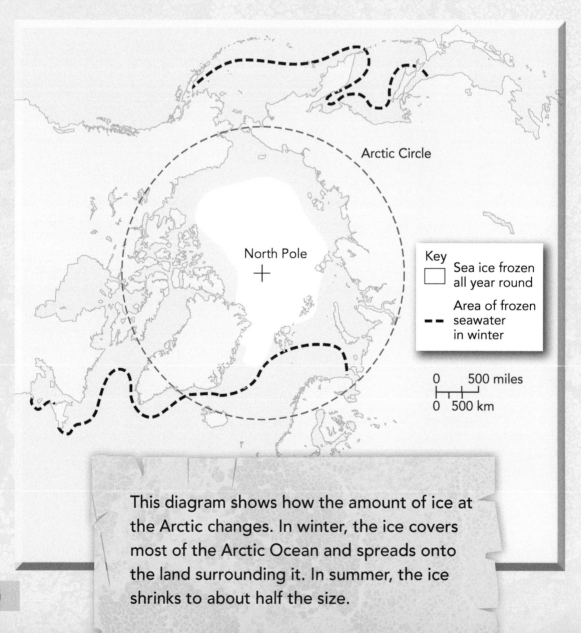

Arctic Circle

North Pole

Key
☐ Sea ice frozen all year round

- - Area of frozen seawater in winter

0   500 miles
0   500 km

This diagram shows how the amount of ice at the Arctic changes. In winter, the ice covers most of the Arctic Ocean and spreads onto the land surrounding it. In summer, the ice shrinks to about half the size.

In summer, some areas of the Arctic look like they might be full of life.

Summer in the Arctic

The Arctic is slightly warmer than the Antarctic, because of warm sea and air **currents**. In summer, plants can grow on the land around the edge of the Arctic. This is because the top layer of earth **thaws**. This means that there is food for animals.

Antarctica

Unlike the Arctic, Antarctica is a huge area of land. It forms one of the world's **continents**. Most of the land is covered all year round by a huge sheet of ice. The ice is up to 14,764 feet (4,500 meters) thick in some places! Only the highest mountains stick out above the ice.

Antarctica is surrounded by the very deep, cold Southern Ocean. In winter, the sea around the land freezes, forming an ice layer up to 6 feet (2 meters) thick. In summer, the ocean melts, but sometimes only the very edges of the land are free of ice.

The Antarctic is incredibly cold.

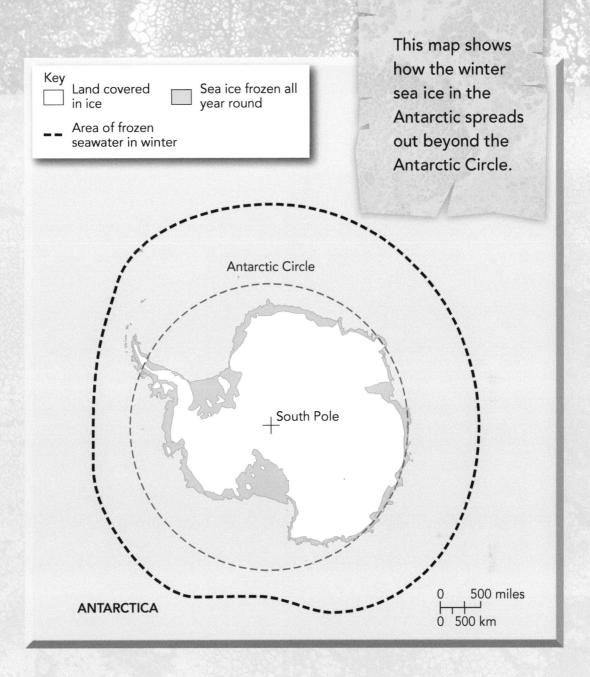

This map shows how the winter sea ice in the Antarctic spreads out beyond the Antarctic Circle.

Key
- ☐ Land covered in ice
- ☐ Sea ice frozen all year round
- – – Area of frozen seawater in winter

Antarctic Circle

+ South Pole

0   500 miles

0   500 km

ANTARCTICA

Antarctic life

There is no proper soil in Antarctica, just tiny bits of gravel. Few types of plants can survive here. There are no plant-eating animals apart from some tiny insects, and no hunting land animals, as there is nothing for them to hunt.

Most animal life in the Antarctic is based in the sea. Some animals come onto the land for resting, **breeding**, and raising their young.

Cold-Loving Plants

In the polar regions, there are some big challenges for plants. It is very cold all year round, often with fierce winds. The short summers mean that plants only have a short time to grow, flower, and make seeds. Arctic soils are very thin and wet. Below the surface, the ground is always frozen. This stops water from draining away from the surface.

In Antarctica, only very simple plants can survive, such as **algae** and moss. Only the Antarctic Peninsula, which juts out of the Antarctic Circle, has flowering plants. However, there are only two types—pearlwort and hair grass.

A kind of algae grows in the Antarctic snow. It colors the snow pink and is sometimes called watermelon snow.

Arctic poppies can turn their heads toward the Sun to catch as much warmth and light as possible.

Arctic plants

In the Arctic, plants—even trees—grow low to the ground to avoid the biting wind. The Arctic willow grows sideways, along the ground, instead of up into the air. Most plants grow very slowly.

Tough trees

A few hardy forests grow around the edge of the Arctic Circle. Pine, spruce, fir, and larch trees have needles. These cope better with frost and snow than leaves.

Animals of the Arctic

An amazing variety of animals live in the Arctic polar region. They have **adapted** to cope with the cold temperatures, the strong winds, the lack of food, and the icy seas.

Walruses have thick layers of fat to help them keep warm.

Fat and fur help many Arctic animals survive the cold. The layer of fat on a caribou can make up about one-sixth of its weight! The Arctic fox's thick fur is very special. In winter, it turns white to **camouflage** the fox in the snow. The fur also has tiny pockets of air in each strand. This helps to protect the fox from the cold.

Perfect polar hunter

Polar bears have fat and waterproof fur to keep them warm. They are camouflaged to help them hunt. They have an excellent sense of smell, and bumps on their feet help them to grip the ice.

Coping with cold

Fish in the Arctic have a special chemical in their blood that prevents it from freezing. Insect eggs can survive the winter buried in the ground. Some birds live in the Arctic in the summer and **migrate** to warmer areas in the winter.

Arctic Food Webs

All living things need **energy** to survive. Plants get their energy from sunlight. They use this to make food for themselves. Some animals eat plants to get their energy. Some animals eat other animals, and some eat a mix of plants and animals. The energy in a **food chain** passes from plant to animal to animal, and so on. A food web is made up of lots of connecting food chains.

Herbivores and carnivores

Plant-eating animals are called herbivores. Arctic herbivores include elk, voles, and snowshoe hares. They are hunted by **predators** such as wolves and brown bears. Animals that eat other animals are called carnivores.

Some animals, like these caribou, **migrate** north to the Arctic in summertime. They come to graze on the summer plants.

Birds such as finches and larks feast on hatching insects in spring. Snowy owls eat lemmings and other small **mammals**, such as voles. Polar bears will eat berries and seabirds if they can't find seals or small whales to eat.

This snowy owl is about to pounce on a small mammal.

A varied diet

Animals that have the widest range of food to eat can survive better than others. This is because they won't starve if one type of food becomes scarce or dies out.

Animals of the Antarctic

Most Antarctic animals live in and around the sea, because the land is so cold and there is little food to be found. Penguins come onto the land to **breed** and raise their chicks. Instead of wings they have flippers, which make them excellent swimmers.

Adapted for the cold

Some Antarctic birds have special **veins** in their feet. This is to stop them from losing heat when they stand on ice. Many types of whales, such as minke whales, live in the Southern Ocean. Whales and seals have thick layers of fat to help them cope with the cold.

Emperor penguins huddle together during the freezing Antarctic winters.

Hunting with sound

Weddell seals can dive over 984 feet (300 meters). They hunt fish using **echolocation**. They do this by making high-pitched squeaks and listening for echoes bouncing back off other animals.

Land dwellers

Only very tiny animals such as mites and springtails live year round on the Antarctic land. Springtails are tiny insects with chemicals in their bodies. These chemicals prevent the springtails from freezing. They can survive temperatures as low as −22 degrees Fahrenheit (−30 degrees Celsius)!

Antarctic Food Webs

Most **food chains** and food webs must start with plants, because they trap **energy** from the Sun. In the Antarctic, there is so little plant life on the land that it does not support many animals. Instead, the plant life is found in the Southern Ocean. Here, tiny, floating plants called **phytoplankton** can capture the Sun's light. These plants are eaten by tiny animals called **zooplankton**.

Krill

Krill, a type of zooplankton, is a very important food source. Fish, birds, seals, and whales all eat krill. Seals and penguins eat fish, and orcas (killer whales) eat seals.

These krill are eating tiny plants in the sea. Many animals eat krill.

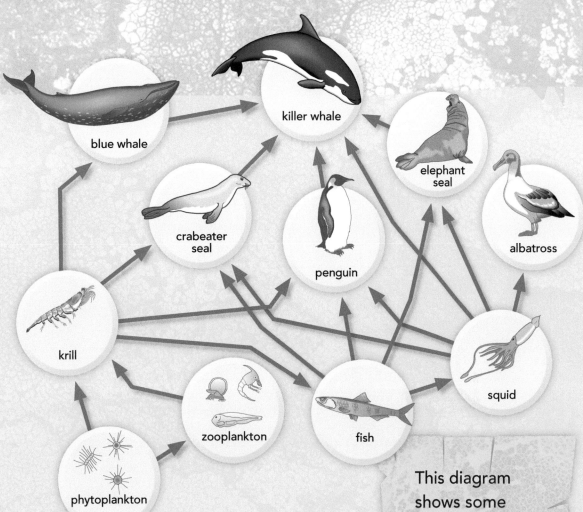

blue whale

killer whale

crabeater seal

penguin

elephant seal

albatross

krill

zooplankton

fish

squid

phytoplankton

On the land, penguin chicks and eggs are at risk. Birds called polar skuas hunt them, looking around for any that are unguarded. Other birds feed on fish, shrimp, and squid from the sea.

This diagram shows some Antarctic food chains linked together to form a food web. The arrows show the movement of energy from one living thing to another.

Wrong name!

Crabeater seals do not eat crabs. In fact, they eat krill, fish, and squid!

People at the Poles

There are no humans living on Antarctica, apart from scientists and tourists who stay for a while and then leave. It is simply too cold and harsh for humans to live there all the time. During the winter, it is impossible to get supplies, such as fresh food, to the Antarctic. Supplies have to be brought in before winter begins.

Scientists in Antarctica live in modern research stations. They come to study things like **climate** and weather patterns.

Living in the Arctic

In the Arctic, there are no humans living around the North **Pole** because there is no land there! However, there are many different people living on the land around the edge of the Arctic Circle. Inuit people live in North America and Greenland. Nenets people live in Siberia. Saami people live in Northern Europe.

It is impossible to grow much food in the Arctic. Instead, people travel across the frozen land and sea to hunt animals such as seal and walrus.

Many Saami people use snowmobiles to help them herd their reindeer.

Old skills

In the past, people had to use animal furs and skins to keep them warm. They learned how to build shelters, such as **igloos**, to keep out of the bad weather. Now, most Arctic people live in modern houses, in modern towns.

Polar Regions at Risk

Very few people live in the Arctic, and only visitors stay in Antarctica. However, the polar regions are under threat from human activity. **Habitats** there are at risk, because even very slight changes can have a big effect on the plants and animals living there.

Global warming, caused by burning coal and oil, is one of the threats to the polar regions. As the planet warms up, more of the ice will melt and there will be less space for animals to live in.

Global warming could be a disaster for polar bears. They use the ice to travel huge distances when they are hunting for food.

Summer vacation?

The amazing polar regions attract tourists. However, even though many tourist companies are careful, litter and waste can end up polluting the area. Also, some people are worried that tourists are getting too close to the wild animals.

Ozone problems

Gases from spray cans and old refrigerators are also causing problems. These gases have destroyed some of the natural **ozone** gas in the air above the Antarctic. This lets more harmful rays from the Sun through, killing some of the **phytoplankton** and **zooplankton** in the Southern Ocean. This means there is less food for sea creatures.

Resources at the Poles

Mining for coal and **minerals** and drilling for oil are not allowed in the Antarctic. However, this is not the case in the Arctic. Oil drilling is a big problem there. Many areas have been damaged by the building of oil rigs and all the roads, pipelines, airports, and power stations that the oil rigs need. Some animals, such as caribou, can no longer **migrate** where they wish. They are stopped by the long oil pipelines that carry the oil.

There are many oil rigs in the Arctic. There is always a risk of oil **pollution**.

Floating fish factories

Enormous factory fishing ships can catch many tons of fish every day. The fish are processed and frozen on board, and some ships can stay at sea for weeks at a time. When people catch more fish from the sea, this means there is less food for other animals, and some fish species may die out.

Largest mine

The Norilsk Nickel mine in Russia is one of the largest mines in the Arctic. Minerals called nickel and palladium are mined there. The mining factories produce huge amounts of a gas called sulphur dioxide. This gas destroys plants and creates a foggy haze in the air.

The Struggle to Survive

With the threats to polar **habitats** increasing, plants and animals are being affected. Scientists have noticed that polar bears are losing weight. There are fewer polar bear cubs being born. More cubs are dying, because their mothers can't feed them properly.

Stop hunting!

Seals were once hunted so much that they nearly became **extinct**. Rules on hunting have changed this, and now numbers are slowly increasing.

In some places in the Arctic, oil pipes have been raised to allow caribou to pass underneath them.

Protecting polar life

There is better news for the Southern Ocean. The **ozone** hole that is affecting **phytoplankton** and **zooplankton** may shrink. This is because many countries have banned the harmful gases that destroy it. In time, the ocean's food supply may return to normal.

Huge **reserves** have been created in the Arctic to protect the special habitat there. These include the Great Arctic Nature Reserve in northern Russia and the Arctic National Wildlife Refuge in Alaska.

Polar Regions in the Future

Habitats in our polar regions are very special places where some amazing plants and animals live. However, these habitats are at risk from human activity. It is up to us to try to save these habitats by changing our activities.

The good news is that there are already people working to save the polar regions. Scientists in Antarctica are working out how best to preserve the Antarctic. New nature **reserves** are creating safe habitats, and new technology can make oil drilling less damaging.

You can help

You can do lots of things to help the polar regions:
- Find out more about them—read books and research web sites.
- Join a conservation group that protects polar regions.
- Adopt an animal that lives in the polar regions.
- Be **energy** wise to help reduce **global warming**.
- Tell your friends and family so they can help, too.

Adopt a polar bear!

The WWF (World Wide Fund for Nature) has a plan where people can adopt polar bears. The money people give to do this is used to help protect polar bears and their habitats.

It is important to protect the polar regions so that these amazing habitats can exist for many years to come.

Glossary

adapt change that helps a plant or animal survive

algae very simple plants that mainly live in water

atmosphere gases surrounding Earth

breed produce young

camouflage color or pattern used to blend into the background

climate weather pattern in a particular part of the world

continent one of Earth's seven large areas of land

current large body of water or mass of air flowing in one direction

desert very dry part of the world that gets very little rainfall

echolocation way of locating objects using sound, used by some animals to find prey

energy power needed to grow, move, and live

extinct no longer existing

food chain series of living things that provide food for each other

global warming increase in Earth's temperature, caused by chemicals in the air trapping the Sun's heat

habitat place where plants and animals live

igloo dome-shaped hut made of blocks of snow

mammal warm-blooded animal that usually has fur or hair. Babies drink milk from their mother.

migrate move from one location to another

mineral substance formed in the earth that is often valuable to people

ozone gas found in Earth's atmosphere

phytoplankton tiny plants living in water

pole top or bottom of Earth

pollution spoiling air, land, or water with harmful things such as plastic garbage

predator animal that hunts and eats other animals

reserve area set aside for the protection of plants and animals

thaw become soft as a result of warming up

vein thin tube that carries blood around the body

zooplankton tiny animals living in water

Find Out More

Books

Ganeri, Anita. *The Polar Regions' Most Amazing Animals.* Chicago: Raintree, 2009.

Kerr, Jim. *Polar Regions* (Earth's Final Frontiers). Chicago: Heinemann Library, 2008.

Newland, Sonya. *Polar Animals* (Saving Wildlife). Mankato, Minn.: Smart Apple Media, 2012.

Pyers, Greg. *Biodiversity of Polar Regions.* New York: Benchmark Books, 2010.

Internet Sites

Facthound offers a safe, fun way to find Internet sites related to this book. All of the sites on Facthound have been researched by our staff.

Here's all you do:

Visit *www.facthound.com*

Type in this code: 9781410945990

Index